C000130369

Peep

by Jodi Gray

Peep was first performed in Bewley's Café Theatre,
Dublin, on 19 February 2018.

Peep

by Jodi Gray

Cast

Caitlin	Alexandra Conlon
May	Emily Fox

Creative Team

Director	Gavin Kostick
Assistant Director	Mollie Molumby
Costume & Set Designer	Ursula McGinn
Light & Sound Designer	John Gunning
Fight Director	Bryan Burroughs
Voice Coach	Cathal Quinn
Producers	Alexandra Conlon & Emily Fox

For Bewley's Café Theatre

Technical & Front of House Manager	Colm Maher
Artistic Director	David Horan
Administration	Iseult Golden

Cast

Alexandra Conlon | Caitlin
Recent theatre work includes *Efficacy84*, as part of
Dublin Fringe Festival 2017, and *Anna Karenina*, a
new adaptation by Marina Carr, directed by Wayne
Jordan at the Abbey Theatre.

Other theatre work includes *Sunder, On Corporation
Street, These Rooms* directed by Louise Lowe (in
collaboration with CoisCéim Dance Theatre); *Last
Words: Proclaiming a Republic* (at the National
Museum of Ireland); *Beyond Barricades, Into the Sun*
(ANU Productions), and *Ladyplay* directed by Davey Kelleher.

Film work includes the short film *Dumped*.

Alexandra graduated from The Lir, National Academy of Dramatic Art
where she performed in productions including *Coop, Tarry Flynn, My
Child* and *O Go My Man*.

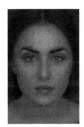

Emily Fox | May
Emily completed her final year of training for the
three-year Bachelor in Acting at The Lir Academy,
Trinity College Dublin in 2016.

Her work with the Lir includes *Spring Awakening*
directed by Selina Cartmell, *In the Next Room; or
the Vibrator Play* directed by David Horan, *The
Cradle Will Rock* and *Agamemnon* both directed by
Wayne Jordan, *Buddleia* directed by Tom Creed,
Once In a Blood Moon – which was devised with
director Annie Ryan, *Sharon's Grave* directed by Conall Morrison,
As You Like It directed by Hilary Wood and Ruth Meehan's short film
*A Minute to Midnigh*t, in which she plays the role of Roisin.

Emily was cast in Season 2 of *Into the Badlands* in 2017.

Creative Team

Jodi Gray | Writer
Plays include *Big Bad* (VAULT Festival 2018); *SSA*, *The Front Room*, *Reach Out and Touch Me*, *You Could Move*, *hookup* and *Affection* (all Outbox Theatre Company, in London and on tour); and shorts for The Miniaturists, Bold Tendencies and the Caravan Theatre. Jodi works extensively in drama schools, including Oxford School of Drama, Royal Central School of Drama and ArtsEd. Short films include *Sidetracked* (dir. Freddie Hall; nominated for Best Writer at Underwire Festival 2015); and *Broken Meats* (dir. Sam Phillips). She is currently on attachment at the Oxford Playhouse as part of their Playmaker scheme, and is Associate Artist with Vanner Collective and Living Record Theatre Company.

Gavin Kostick | Director
Gavin is an internationally produced, award-winning playwright. As director he has worked on a number of shows and especially with Tenderfoot (Youth Arts) at the Civic, Tallaght, working annually with young writers for the stage. Gavin is the Literary Manager of Fishamble: The New Play Company, Tutor in Dramaturgy at The Lir Academy and Tutor in Playwrighting at Trinity College, Dublin.

Mollie Molumby | Assistant Director
Mollie is a director and theatre maker based in Dublin. She studied Drama at Trinity College Dublin, and trained in Drama Facilitation with Youth Theatre Ireland. Mollie is the artistic director of Bombinate Theatre, a collective of emerging artists making plays for families and young audiences. She directed Bombinate's debut production *Half Light* (Dublin Fringe 2016, First Fortnight 2017, national tour 2018), winner of the First Fortnight Award and nominated for Best Ensemble at Dublin Fringe 2016.

Ursula McGinn | Costume & Set Designer
Ursula is a theatre-maker working as a director, designer and stage manager. Recent design credits include *Half Light* (Dublin Fringe 2016, First Fortnight 2017, Irish national tour 2018); *King Lear* (Gaiety School of Acting, 2017); and *Sunny Dayz* (Samuel Beckett Theatre 2017). Ursula is a co-founder of Bombinate Theatre, an award-winning collective of emerging theatre makers, creating work for families and young audiences. She is an alumna of Dublin Youth Theatre and holds a BA in Drama and Theatre Studies from Trinity College.

John Gunning | Light & Sound Designer
John is an alumnus of Dublin Youth Theatre and The Lir Academy. He is participant of Rough Magic's 9th SEEDS programme and a founding member of Malaprop Theatre (Recipients Spirit of Dublin Fringe 2015, The Georganne Aldrich Heller Award 2017). Lighting design includes *Everything Not Saved* (Project Arts Centre); *Jericho* (Bewley's Café Theatre); *BlackCatfishMusketeer, Love+* (Summerhall Festival); *The Egg Is a Lonely Hunter* (Project Arts Centre); *Flynn* (Peacock); *Running Blind* (Smock Alley); and *Eamonn* (*From Menswear*) (Mick Lally Theatre). Sound design includes *Yen* and *Grimly Handsome* (Lir Academy); *McKenna's Fort* (The New Theatre) and *The Bells Of* (Theatre Upstairs). Video design includes *Jericho* (Bewley's Cafè Theatre) with Claire O'Reilly.

Thank You

Fishamble: The New Play Company, Bewley's Café Theatre, Nick Hern Books, Paul Livingstone, Kyle Cheldon Barnett, Smock Alley Theatre, Ali Fox, Cathal Quinn, Bryan Burroughs, Adam Whelehan, Stephen Whelehan & David Donavan.

Supported By

Dublin FringeLAB, Irish Theatre Institute.

PEEP

Jodi Gray

Peep was first seen as a short play at The Miniaturists 45, Arcola Theatre, London, on 9 February 2014. The cast was as follows:

CAITLIN	Crissy O Donovan
MAY	Charlotte Duffy
Director	Jemima James

A work-in-progress extract of the play was also seen at Collaborations Festival at the Smock Alley Theatre, Dublin, on 26 February 2015, with technical support by Aidan Crowe.

Acknowledgements

First off, this play would never have seen the light of day if not for two wonderful women, Charlotte Duffy and Crissy O Donovan. I owe them both rather a lot. And all the thanks to Jemima James who leapt aboard as director and steered us right.

Praise be to The Miniaturists (at that time curated by Will Bourdillon and Declan Feenan, but honourable mentions for Flavia Fraser-Cannon, Steve King and Stephen Sharkey), not just for giving this play its first public outing, but for all the other plays, and being a wonderful company.

Big loves to all at Nick Hern Books: Siân Mayhall-Purvis, Sarah Liisa Wilkinson, Matt Applewhite, John O'Donovan, Marcelo Dos Santos, Tim Digby-Bell, Tamara von Werthern, Jon Barton, Ian Higham, Robin Booth, Jane Maud and Nick Hern.

Huge gratitude to Gavin Kostick, Alexandra Conlon, Emily Fox and Mollie Molumby, who breathed new life, depth and lols into *Peep* – and found it a home, finally, in its hometown; and thanks, therefore, to Bewley's for being it.

General round-up of specific thanks for their support, inspiration and patience during *Peep*'s gestation: Ben Buratta, Barry Fitzgerald, Elle Hewitt, Declan Feenan (again), Steve King (again), Maud Dromgoole, Bella Gibbins, Louise Marwood, Deirdre McLaughlin, Kenny Emson and Ben Musgrave, Sophie Clark, Sammy Collins, Charlotte Peach, Matt Applewhite and Sarah Liisa Wilkinson (again), the staff and students at the Oxford School of Drama, the alumni of Outbox Theatre – and my family (but especially my various parents and siblings, and of those especially the original ones: Kim, Steve, Benn and Charlie).

There are definitely others, but, frankly, this has gone on long enough.

J.G.

For all the exes

(keep your curtains closed)

Characters

CAITLIN, *Dublin, mid- to late-twenties*
MAY, *Dublin, mid- to late-twenties*

Note

The play is set in Dublin, present day.

Each scene takes place a number of weeks after the last, and it's always the middle of the night.

The holiday/birthday decorations that appear after Scene One can be altered to better suit the time of year at which the play is performed, although there should never be any in Scene One.

A 'blank' line indicates a change of focus to, or non-verbal cue for, that character.

An ellipsis (…) indicates a beat or a pause.

A forward slash (/) indicates the point at which the next speaker interrupts.

This text went to press before the end of rehearsals and so may differ slightly from the play as performed.

1.

MAY *and* CAITLIN, *both looking through the window ahead with binoculars. They sit in picnic chairs.* MAY*'s is probably more brightly coloured than* CAITLIN*'s. Both have bottles of water beside them,* MAY *has a rucksack as well beside her. Just looking.*

MAY   What time's it?

CAITLIN   (*Quick, precise look at her watch.*) Almost midnight.

MAY   Almost midnight?

CAITLIN   Getting late, boys, getting late.

MAY   Was your toilet break not at half past?

CAITLIN   What?

MAY   Were you not on for a toilet break at half past eleven?

CAITLIN   Don't need it.

MAY   Don't need it. Well. Really? Don't ya?

             Not need a little weewee there?

CAITLIN   No I don't need a little fuckin weewee.

             …

             MAY, *bit bored, turns her binoculars on* CAITLIN.

MAY   You're getting a line.

CAITLIN   What?

MAY   Like a squinty line here – (*Between her eyebrows.*) like a peepin squinty –

CAITLIN   I am not.

MAY   From all the peepin. Great. Means I'll be getting
            one next. Better order in some Olay or something.
            Bit of the old L'Oréal because I'm worth it thank
            you very much.

CAITLIN   Will you shuddup for a minute? Honest to god.

MAY

CAITLIN   Tryinta concentrate.

MAY   Exactly your problem, I'd say. (*Indicates the line
            again.*)

CAITLIN

MAY   Only trying to help.

CAITLIN   Fuck's sake. Have I taught you nothing?

MAY   I dunno.

CAITLIN   Gotta keep your head in the game, haven't you.

MAY   And my eyes on the prize.

CAITLIN   You know it. (*Gestures out of the window.*)

MAY   I do. Yes. The game – (*Gestures the two of them.*)
            The prize – (*Gestures the window.*)

CAITLIN   Okay then?

MAY   Oh yes.

            …

            So it's not midnight-snack time yet?

CAITLIN   No.

MAY   Can hear my own stomach. It's roaring. You hear
            that?

CAITLIN   All I hear is your flappin face.

MAY   Roaring.

CAITLIN   You got your water?

MAY   Right here.

CAITLIN   Got your supplies?

MAY   Present and correct.

CAITLIN   So stop moaning and eat something. Jesus. Not your fuckin mother.

MAY   Ho-ho you're not. No you are not. (*Looking in the rucksack by her side.*) You not want anything?

CAITLIN   Ha. Not from you.

MAY   And so what's that meant to mean?

CAITLIN   I'm not hungry.

MAY   You think I'll poison you. You think I'm gonna – is that it?

CAITLIN   I think whatever I want to.

MAY   Oh yeah.

CAITLIN   Think whatever I like about you.

MAY   Oh right. What's that then? Whaddya thinking about me?

          …

CAITLIN   Not fuckin much, May. Not much at all.

MAY   Oh well that's very nice. That's charming. 'Not much.'

CAITLIN   I think. What I like. Yeah?

MAY   Eating's good though, Cait. Isn't it. Helps keep the mind tickin over. Helps with the focus.

CAITLIN   Right you are.

          MAY *is opening a huge bag of Tangy Cheese Doritos.*

MAY   Gotta keep the strength up.

CAITLIN   Honest to god, will ya not just put something in your fuckin mouth?

MAY

            MAY *takes a massive handful of Doritos and shoves them into her mouth, crunching as loudly as she can, looking at* CAITLIN *all the while. Crumbs everywhere.*

            (*Through a mouthful.*) Are you sure you don't want some? They're delicious.

CAITLIN   Fuckin stink.

MAY   Mm. Delicious. (*Shoves a few more in.*)

CAITLIN   Fuckin stinks in here.

MAY   Good for the mind, good for the soul.

CAITLIN   Did you ever look at yourself?

MAY   I'm fine.

CAITLIN   Look at yourself.

MAY   Unbelievable. I can't believe you'd –

            You wanna start that, Cait? You want to start 'lookin at ourselves'?

CAITLIN

MAY   Didn't think so, did I. That way madness, eh. That's the way it lies.

            MAY *goes for another handful of Doritos and* CAITLIN –

CAITLIN   GET TO FUCK.

            – *whacks the bag out of her hand, away from them both. Doritos everywhere.*

            MAY *looks at the bag. It's too far to reach without leaving her spot at the window. Panics a bit. Gives up.*

MAY   Oh well. Had enough now, anyway.

CAITLIN   Yeah yeah.

MAY   Had my fill.

CAITLIN   That's good, yeah.

MAY   Delicious, but.

             …

CAITLIN   I'm sorry for throwing your Doritos.

MAY

CAITLIN   I am.

MAY   Well.

CAITLIN   No because. I know we've talked about – my
             temper.

MAY   We have.

CAITLIN   And I know I said I'd make an effort not to take
             out my stress and troubles on you.

MAY   Because it's not really fair, is it.

CAITLIN   No.

MAY   Because it's not my fault we're here.

CAITLIN   It isn't.

MAY   We know who's at fault, don't we. We're in this,
             aren't we, you said that we have to remember that
             we're in this –

CAITLIN   Together.

MAY   Okay. So.

CAITLIN   So. As I say. I apologise.

MAY   S'okay.

             …

CAITLIN   You have to say it.

MAY

CAITLIN   'I accept your' – you have to say it.

MAY   Oh yeah, that's the one. I accept your apology.

CAITLIN   Great now. That's. Okay.

            But you'd have to admit you were deliberately
            gettin at me then.

MAY   Wasn't –

CAITLIN   No no. Come on. You were purposefully baiting me.

MAY   I might have been. A little.

CAITLIN   Which, you know. Hurts a bit. Actually.

MAY   Ah no, Cait.

CAITLIN   No it's fine.

MAY   Then look – I apologise. For baiting you. It was
            a bad thing to do and I didn't mean any harm and
            I was just. Ahm. I was just.

CAITLIN   'Acting out for attention.'

MAY   Right, I apologise and I was just acting out for
            attention.

CAITLIN   And I accept your apology. There. Great.

            …

MAY   What was in that package then?

CAITLIN

MAY   The one I signed for. Carried up a bunch of stairs
            for ya?

CAITLIN   Ah right, so. Nothin really.

MAY   Heavy for nothin.

CAITLIN   Well. I don't know what to tell ya.

MAY	Is it a surprise, Cait?
	…
CAITLIN	If you like. If you behave.
MAY	Ah great. Love surprises.
	…
	Is it a good surprise?
CAITLIN	If you BEHAVE I said.
MAY	Gotcha.
	…
	What if we went to the pub? Had a little pint at the pub.
CAITLIN	
MAY	We could.
CAITLIN	We could, we could, but I'd say the minute we put foot to pavement he'd be back.
MAY	Yeah.
CAITLIN	He'd be home then and we'd be – fuck. Can you imagine it? Stuck out there and himself up the stairs and home. And we're missing it. Do you wanna miss it?
MAY	Not much I don't. I would not want to miss that.
	…
CAITLIN	Been a while though, eh?
MAY	Y'what?
CAITLIN	Little pint. Been a while.
MAY	Oh yeah.
CAITLIN	Little drink, little dance.
MAY	Couldn't tell ya how long. Couldn't hazard a guess, probably.

CAITLIN   I loved a dance.

MAY   You're joking.

CAITLIN   I'm not.

MAY   Can't see you as a dancer.

CAITLIN   I danced. Oh, I danced.

MAY   Never much for dancing, me.

CAITLIN   Could show you some shapes.

MAY   Oh yeah.

CAITLIN   Teach you some moves some time.

MAY   Dunno about that, Cait. Not much of a mover.

CAITLIN   That's a shame.

MAY   I don't mind. I was always that one getting bollixed in the corner with the boys, chatting shite to some poor soul.

CAITLIN   Oh well I can see that about ya. Chatting the shite.

MAY   Oh yes.

CAITLIN   Ha.

MAY   Worked though. Seemed to. Usually ended up going home with one lad or other, so. Seemed to work for me.

CAITLIN   Bit slaggy, no?

MAY   Um, no –

CAITLIN   Sounds a bit slaggy if you ask me.

MAY   Wasn't asking.

CAITLIN   I just call it how I see it.

MAY   I didn't ask you to.

CAITLIN   You don't have to listen.

MAY	Anyway, what about you, jiggling away on the dancefloor. Bumping and grinding and moving away. What was all that for?
CAITLIN	For dancin –
MAY	For attention-grabbing. For finding someone. That's what.
CAITLIN	Dance like no one's watching, that was me.
MAY	Oh yeah.
CAITLIN	Not for grabbing anything. Wasn't like that.
MAY	Whatever you say.
CAITLIN	The fuck you on about.
MAY	I just call it like I see it.
	…
CAITLIN	Sometimes, I'd say, you seem nearly – ungrateful.
MAY	Ungrateful?
CAITLIN	That's what it feels like sometimes. I'm only – okay? Saying.
	…
MAY	You didn't have to come and find me.
CAITLIN	What now?
MAY	You didn't have to tell me.
CAITLIN	'Didn't have to' – ?
MAY	I mean – why did you do that?
CAITLIN	What?
MAY	Were ya lonely? Getting lonesome up here by yourself. Was that it?
CAITLIN	I am on a knife's edge right now, May, I swear –

MAY   Because that's the only thing I can think. You were
             turning into a lonely, bitter old bitch and you
             wanted a friend.

             So. That's why. Why, I think you came down / and
             told me and –

CAITLIN   You deserved to know.

MAY   Pardon me?

CAITLIN   I came to find ya because you deserved to know.

MAY   You'd never even met me, how'd you know what
             I deserved or didn't or –

CAITLIN   BECAUSE WE ALL DESERVE TO KNOW.

             Okay? That's how. Cuz we all deserve that at
             least. Doesn't matter what –

             It's humiliating otherwise. It's just. You know?
             Awful.

             …

MAY   How long did you know?

CAITLIN

MAY   How long did you know he was messin me
             around? Before you told me.

CAITLIN   Only.

MAY   Truths.

CAITLIN   Couple of weeks. Maybe three.

             I couldn't tell at first if it was the same – if you
             were the same every time.

MAY   Oh, for god's sake –

CAITLIN   No, cuz listen cuz you used to do so many different
             things with your hair, amazing like – up or down or
             sideways or sometimes even one time it looked like
             you'd chopped it all off but it was all only clips or
             grips or spray or something – I'm guessing.

MAY	I did do that.
CAITLIN	And outfits like I couldn't even believe sometimes, the things you'd hang off yourself like some glamourpuss, like some, I don't know.
MAY	Model?
CAITLIN	A bit like a model, yeah. Not like a – maybe not catwalk, like, but maybe one of them catalogues, Littlewoods or. Argos or.
	...
MAY	Glamourpuss, was I.
CAITLIN	I have to say. You were.
MAY	I tell ya something?
CAITLIN	
MAY	All on the credit cards.
CAITLIN	No.
MAY	Oops.
CAITLIN	That's some risk.
MAY	Well.
CAITLIN	That's some risky business. Didn't have you down for that.
MAY	I wanted to be – impressive, I think. You're called a lot of things over the years, but I'd never been all that impressive. And he made me want to be it.
CAITLIN	Risky.
MAY	Looking back.
CAITLIN	So. Anyway. I couldn't tell for a while that it was you every time. For a while. And I had to make sure you weren't just a one-night thing, didn't I?
MAY	So you waited. To tell me.
CAITLIN	I did.

MAY   Laughin at me makin a fool of myself –

             …

CAITLIN   Bet you wish you'd never met him, though.

MAY

CAITLIN   Wish you'd never met him, I bet. That's what
             you wish.

MAY   I wish I'd never met you.

CAITLIN

MAY   Wish I'd never met ya and I didn't know.

CAITLIN   I could've killed him. Hated him that much. For
             a while there I thought I really thought I might.

MAY   You would not.

CAITLIN   I might.

MAY   You wouldn't even dare.

CAITLIN   Still crosses my mind from time to time, I have to
             say. Only daydreams, like.

             …

MAY   I was gonna kill you. Not wi poison, mind. If
             I killed ya, you'd know about it.

CAITLIN   Pff.

MAY   I still might.

             MAY*'s attention caught out of the window.*

CAITLIN   I'm not scared of you.

MAY   Quiet.

CAITLIN   Think I am? I'll just kill yas both. I'm not bothered.

MAY   Will you shuddup –

CAITLIN   Don't you –

MAY   – and look.

CAITLIN	What. Fuck.
MAY	Didn't even see the car park up, did you?
CAITLIN	How did we miss it? Where's the – the car's not even there, May.
MAY	Sneaky little so-and-so.
CAITLIN	Oh, okay now – look at him, he's langered. Never drank and driven, did he.
MAY	Nope. Always conscientious in that respect.
CAITLIN	Fuck fuck fuck this is what happens when you don't keep your fuckin head in the game.

…

	He's had a haircut hasn't he.
MAY	It's a bit.
CAITLIN	Makes him look. / Old.
MAY	Younger.

…

	Always loved him in that T-shirt.
CAITLIN	Saw you in that T-shirt one morning, didn't I.
MAY	You will have, yeah.
CAITLIN	And over to the stereo, three two one –
MAY	Whaddya think he's going for tonight?
CAITLIN	Fleetwood Mac?
MAY	Oh, The Mac. Classic.
CAITLIN	Or – no, he's got a little jig on there.
MAY	Never jigged to The Mac. Maybe Rihanna?
CAITLIN	No. Really?
MAY	Oh yeah – did you never – ?

CAITLIN   No no. Rihanna though?

MAY   I think I loaned him the CD, actually –

CAITLIN   And there she is. What's her name?

MAY   Oh, boo, her. That'll be Mizz Brigid Anna
       Katherine Fitzgerald, lives in Dublin, originally
       from Tullow, County Carlow, she's one brother,
       two sisters, and we've no mutual friends – though
       that's no surprise, wha.

CAITLIN   That's a terrifyin amount of information you have
          on the girl.

MAY   Sláinte, Facebook. So what'll this be then? Two. /
       Three –

CAITLIN   Date three, yeah. Poor girl. I mean, at least you
          can definitely tell it's her. That's the second time
          we've seen that dress, if I'm not much mistaken.

MAY   She's filth – she's no shame, that one.

       CAITLIN *starts to wind* MAY *up.*

CAITLIN   (*Re: him.*) Oh dear, May.

MAY   Is that dancing?

CAITLIN   It is.

MAY   She's dancing with him.

CAITLIN   To your CD.

MAY   To my – She's fuckin dancing with him (scuse me)
       to my fuckin CD (scuse me twice).

CAITLIN   That bitch.

MAY   She's – is that a striptease?

CAITLIN   My god.

MAY   Is she stripping now?

CAITLIN   Not even any knickers, now that's a dreadful
           striptease, you'd have to admit. Ruins the mystery
           if there's no knickers.

MAY   What is she DOING that is HORRIFIC doesn't
           she know that people can SEE HER?

CAITLIN   To be fair to her, he seems to quite like it.

MAY   Oh and there we go, straight down to it.

CAITLIN   As ever. What a fuckin surprise.

MAY   (*Calling out.*) You ever heard of foreplay? Did ya
           not hear about it?

CAITLIN   Tsch. No.

MAY   Um, no. Not likely.

CAITLIN   And – she's ripped his T-shirt. Brigid Fitzgerald
           has ripped his fucking top.

MAY   For fuck's SAKE. (*Maybe kicks or grabs her chair
           and bashes it about a bit.*) Scuse me.

           …

           I loved that T-shirt. It smelled soft. Do you know
           what I mean? Smelled like soft.

           …

CAITLIN   He should really think about investing in some
           curtains.

MAY   Some kind of a blind maybe.

CAITLIN   Ha.

           MAY *looks at* CAITLIN.

MAY   Will we invite her round then?

2.

The flat's a little more lived-in, especially round MAY*'s chair.
There's a new banner or string of bunting across a corner of the
room that reads 'HAPPY BIRTHDAY CAITLIN!', with bright
fresh balloons tied either end.*

CAITLIN*'s holding open the door, we maybe hear footsteps –
running – and another door, off, slam.*

MAY	Well. Now you've done it.
CAITLIN	Excuse me I've done what now?
MAY	Opened the door and let her run off!
CAITLIN	Well, she seemed a little upset, May, didn't you think?
MAY	Told ya we needed precautions. Shoulda blindfolded her on the way up. Or an oath we shoulda made her do an oath!
CAITLIN	We're not wee boys, May –
MAY	Kept the flippin door shut at least.
CAITLIN	We're not shuttin anyone up anywhere, May, you hear me? Do ya?
MAY	Something to make sure, Cait. That's all.
CAITLIN	Look. You have to want to be here, wouldn't you say. It has to be a choice you make yourself. And it has to be your own decision to stay. Otherwise there's no dedication. No heart. And what are we if not dedicated? And what have we if no heart.
MAY	I'm dedicated.
CAITLIN	You are.
MAY	I've the heart.
CAITLIN	Well, you coulda had some heart for her, May. It's a helluva shock, you must remember that.

MAY	I always think, you know. That it was all of a sudden the knowing / that you'd seen –
CAITLIN	We're only telling the truth, now, May, don't these girls deserve the truth?
MAY	No but I'm thinkin of when I'd come round that first time, and what wrecked me head most was thinkin about how *you'd* seen me. I have to say, I did feel very weird about that.
CAITLIN	What's your problem, caller?
MAY	Probably that was what she was so upset about. Brigid, I mean. About how me and you were watchin.
CAITLIN	Ummm – probably it was the fact that he'd been secretly videoing it all, May, no?
MAY	'Video'! All right there, Granny, how's the eighties treating you.
CAITLIN	Fuck off.
MAY	She was definitely more mental about us *seeing* her than him *filming* her, like, wasn't she?
CAITLIN	And what about you going on about it – 'Oh and without your knowledge, Brigid, imagine that – all your most intimate moments, Brigid' –
MAY	Oh but we seen right up her 'Intimate Moment' that one time, didn't we –
CAITLIN	I'm saying you didn't have to go on about exactly how much we'd seen.
MAY	So maybe she shouldnta DONE everything then. Maybe. Then maybe we wouldnta SEEN so much. He never wanted that dirty stuff before.
CAITLIN	Just cuz he never asked *you* doesn't mean he didn't want it.
MAY	He doesn't like it – that filth, he doesn't want it.

CAITLIN   You didn't have to treat her so judgemental, May, it's – it's fuckin cruel, what it is – 'We were thinking maybe it's time for a wee trim, Brigid, HAWHAW – '

MAY   Doesn't even sound at all like me – I don't SOUND like that.

CAITLIN   Sound like that to me. Whiney. Whinnying and. Like a donkey sometimes.

MAY   Oh right donkey now is it?

CAITLIN   Sometimes.

MAY   You wish.

CAITLIN

MAY

CAITLIN

MAY   And anyway what's all that you're on about being watched all the time – that was gas so.

CAITLIN   Gas, yeah.

MAY   About everybody looking at ya –

CAITLIN   That's nothing.

MAY   – and being safe up here –

CAITLIN   I was saying that for her –

MAY   Mm, I don't think so, Cait, that sounded like weirdo talk to me –

CAITLIN   I'm saying that to make her feel better about the being watched by us, and better about being here because up here we're safe –

MAY   Sounded almost like you're maybe a bit – *paranoid* maybe.

CAITLIN   So she knows we're safe up here.

MAY   Maybe even a little bit scared or something,
             I don't know.

CAITLIN   THAT'S SHITE NOW, MAY.

MAY   OKAY, so – what then?

             …

CAITLIN   There was a golden time in my life before you,
             May, if you can imagine that – oh those salad
             fuckin days before YOU and your constant
             bobble-heading, mind-numbing –

             And in those days I'd only seen him, like, about
             the courtyard, you know, bumped into him at the
             gate once or twice, exchanged maybe a 'hello' –
             but I'd no notion that he lived right – (*Gestures
             out of the window.*) I'd no idea till I was round
             there, till I looked out of his window and found
             myself lookin straight into my very own.

MAY   That woulda been a shocker.

CAITLIN   And – then I'm back here and safe home and I'm
             graspin – Caitlin, any one of your neighbours
             coulda seen you over there. If they were to look out
             and – not the same exact sight lines, but. Coulda
             been anyone could see what was happening.

             But nobody didn't do – didn't anybody do –
             anythin.

MAY   Like, so it coulda been anyone was watching me.
             Whenever I was over in there?

CAITLIN   It could.

MAY   That pure gives me the creeps, Cait.

CAITLIN   As it should, May.

MAY   Do you know what?

CAITLIN   What, May?

MAY	And, bear with me, but, I'm just makin some connections here.
	Wasn't it they were looking at us all the time anyway?
CAITLIN	Yes May.
MAY	Lads always eyeing us when we're down the town.
CAITLIN	Taking looks for themselves without even asking. And they take it anyway.
MAY	Lookin greedy at us, with all sorts of filthy imaginings of what they could do.
CAITLIN	And isn't it those very thoughts we feel creepin over us when we walk ourselves home at nights?
MAY	It is.
CAITLIN	That's why we're doin this, May. Remember?
MAY	It's fair droppin into place, here – like, I know you've talked me through it but if I'm honest I never hundred-per-cent got it before.
CAITLIN	So then: number one.
MAY	We take ourselves away up here from all the looking.
CAITLIN	Up here away from the eyes. Number two: we take back the looking for ourselves and we watch that fucker. That fucker. Thinks he can take it from us? Thinks he has us? But there we have him.
MAY	And number three. We watch over the girls.
CAITLIN	We watch over those girls he's messin, we tell them all what he truly is. Till he's so alone that there's barely a speck of him left.
	All of them. Till the last one.
MAY	Till the very last one.
CAITLIN	That's us then?

MAY   That's us.

            …

            I hate that Brigid, that shameless bitch.

CAITLIN   She was a joke, May, that girl.

MAY   She'd not the dedication, Cait.

CAITLIN   No fuckin – None.

MAY   You could tell that straight off.

CAITLIN   She won't tell, May. Cuz nobody'd care. And she
            won't be coming back to us either, but ya know?
            That's okay. Don't need her.

            …

MAY   I came back, Cait, didn't I.

CAITLIN   You did. Unfortunately for me.

MAY   Ah – fortunately unfortunately.

            *They're settled back in for a usual night of
            watching.*

CAITLIN   Oh, em, just while I think about it, did any
            package arrive today for me?

MAY   I don't know.

CAITLIN   You've just been downstairs, haven't ya?

MAY   I wasn't really lookin, Cait. Nothin jumped out
            at me.

CAITLIN   Okay. That's okay. You'll remember to look next
            time you're down there?

MAY   I will.

CAITLIN   Great then.

            A long moment.

MAY   I really feel like we've turned a corner here
            tonight, Cait, I have to say.

CAITLIN   Oh yeah?

MAY	Yeah, cuz. You said. You were sayin just then about that Dirty Brigid and how she's a joke.
CAITLIN	Not a very fuckin good one, but a joke nevertheless, ha?
MAY	So that must mean I'm no joke to you any more. Like you take me serious, like a real contender.
CAITLIN	A fuckin what?
MAY	Ah, ya know what I mean.
	…
CAITLIN	I will say that you're an easy girl to underestimate.
MAY	I knew it. I knew I'd get ya to like me.
CAITLIN	You'll do well to remember that this is simply a temporary and mutually beneficial business arrangement.
MAY	Only a matter of time.
CAITLIN	That's enough now.
MAY	Maybe I'll just keep on talkin till I break ya. I reckon I could probly do that.
CAITLIN	
MAY	I mean, I can just keep on fillin the silences with words and thoughts and feelings and thoughts, if that's how you want to play it –
CAITLIN	
MAY	I AM NOT MADE OF STONE.
CAITLIN	The car's pulling up, May –
	MAY *turns, binoculars up to her face as if by magic*.
MAY	I know.
CAITLIN	Who's that gettin out of the car?
MAY	Is it the mammy one back again?

CAITLIN   Oh you're jokin. Is it Gráinne, her name?

MAY   Gráinne McGonagle. What a mouthful that is.

CAITLIN   Suits her down to the ground, no?

MAY   What is it you'd call that, Cait? There's a word for that mammy-ness about her. That kinda accommodating look she has.

CAITLIN   Homely, is it?

MAY   Yeah, it's somethin like that.

CAITLIN   Jesus. I did not see her sticking around.

MAY   Is that another cake box?

CAITLIN   What the actual fuck.

MAY   Oh but he'll get awful fat, she keeps bringing them cakes over, won't he?

CAITLIN   I always thought he'd run to fat, given the opportunity.

MAY   Well that'd be a terrible waste of a good body.

CAITLIN   You think he's a good body?

MAY   I think it's lovely.

CAITLIN   Umh.

MAY   Not you, Cait?

CAITLIN   I think I thought he'd feel different – you know, when we actually.

MAY   I always thought he felt just lovely.

CAITLIN   When he touched me, I'd just – imagined it completely different.

             …

MAY   What's happening? They take the stairs, do you think? Gettin up their appetites – ha?

             You all right, Cait?

CAITLIN   I'm fine, bit light-headed is all.

MAY   Sure?

CAITLIN   Yes.

MAY   Here they come, and ladies first.

           …

           Bit of mood lighting, is it? Fair enough, I'd say
           she'd be better lookin in the dark, wouldn't she?

CAITLIN   What's he at there, May?

MAY   Hey – looks like maybe he actually heard us about
           the foreplay, Cait! Wouldn't that be somethin?

CAITLIN   What's he doin?

MAY   Looks like he's havin a bit of the 'aul cake'.

CAITLIN   (Disgusting.)

MAY   What're you sayin?

CAITLIN   I do *not* understand all that fuss she's makin.

MAY   What?

CAITLIN   All this – (*Does a squirmy, writhing sort of
           movement.*) It's not real. I mean, nobody's havin
           that much fun.

MAY   Sometimes I feel awful sorry for you.

CAITLIN   It's *ridiculous* –

MAY   Okay there –

CAITLIN   – and there'll be CRUMBS EVERYWHERE.

           …

MAY   Wow.

CAITLIN   I'm sorry.

MAY   And I mean I accept your apology, but –

           …

CAITLIN   She needs to know, May.

MAY   She does.

CAITLIN   It's not real and she needs to know that.

MAY   So – ?

CAITLIN   So – ?

MAY   Tomorrow morning, then?

CAITLIN   Tomorrow morning.

3.

*There's a new picnic chair. Next to it is, maybe, some stuff
including some knitting needles and wool, something almost
knitted hanging off the needles. The banner now reads 'HAPPY
BIRTHD-Y MAY', where the 'A' has fallen off and with 'MAY'
badly and obviously covering the word 'CAITLIN'. The banner
itself is looking pretty sad and droopy, the balloons either side
totally deflated.*

*There's a pizza box and a massive bottle of Coca-Cola by
MAY's feet and a Bag-for-Life filled quite obviously with
tampons by her side.*

MAY   I'm sayin you know like I walk out the door and
        I'm suddenly all of a sudden like – where'm I
        gonna bulk-buy Tampax and painkillers almost
        midnight? You know? This could be tricky.

CAITLIN   Shit – okay, May –

MAY   Wait, you gotta hear this though, Cait, it's brilliant
        – So then I goes Ah yeah there's that all-night
        garage. Brilliant. And it's only right next to the –

CAITLIN   May I have to stop ya / there –

MAY   Seriously, will ya not just let me TELL IT.

CAITLIN

MAY   Thank You. Where was I? Oh yeah – And it's
               only right next to the *pizza place*, and how could
               I murder a Sloppy Giuseppe and a gallon of full-
               flippin-fat Cokey-Cola and what of a chicken-wings
               meal deal and sure couldn't Cait and Mammy
               Gráinne as well being that I'm on a GIRLY
               MISSION for GIRLY PRODUCTS (you're
               welcome, by the way). So, I goes in. I orders.
               Sloppy, Coke, chuh-ICKEN. I'll be back. I'll be
               right back I'm just nippin over the – he gets it he
               understands, probly smell the – the menstrual – the
               hormones off me. Probly he knows.

               And I go over pushin on the door and the guy's
               like – Shutsorry. And I'm going – he's through the
               window through the after-hours hatch – I'm going
               What now? D-Head? Shutsorry.
               Tellmewhatyouwant. I'llgetyouwhatyouwant.

               And I'm lookin. At the hatch. At the – you know
               the little slot thingy. Where you put your. And by
               this time there's truckers and taxi drivers and more
               truckers all queueing up behind waiting to pay for
               the petrol. So.

               I NEED SOME PAINKILLERS AND ALL
               YOUR TAMPAX.

CAITLIN

MAY   *Wait –*

CAITLIN

MAY   I WANT ALL THE TAMPAX YOU HAVE. And
               he's dying, your wee one on the hatch. He's dyin.
               He goes – small voice – little voice – They won't
               fit. YOU WHAT? I goes. We only got the big packs.
               They will not fit. Lookin at the slot. SURE THAT'S
               GRAND. Says I. GOT ME BAG-FOR-LIFE.

And I'm shaking it. And he's stood there, and *I* go,
Open the flippin box and feed those babies through.
And he does. Thirteen boxes and he – opens em on
up and feeds em on through.

...

CAITLIN   Are ya finished?

MAY   Well I was expecting a bit more of a reaction if
            I'm honest.

CAITLIN   I've to tell you somethin.

MAY   So, ah, where *is* Mammy Gráinne?

CAITLIN   May, now, don't go overreacting here. It seems
            she took some pills –

MAY   IT 'SEEMS' SHE TOOK SOME –

CAITLIN   She's fine, she'll not die.

MAY   Oh she won't?

CAITLIN   No.

MAY   And how'd you diagnose that, then, doctor?

CAITLIN   Well we'd only three Nurofen left in the box,
            didn't we, so she just went and necked a bunch of
            your B-vitamin-formula shite.

MAY   Well that's annoyin, they're not cheap those.

CAITLIN   In truth I doubt she'll have achieved much more
            than a fierce bout of constipation.

MAY   Ooph, cry for help, was it?

CAITLIN   She called the fuckin ambulance herself, if you
            can believe that.

MAY   Jays but that's a sad story, wha.

CAITLIN   Waited for the blue flashin lights at the window and
            took herself off downstairs. It was all quite – unreal.

MAY   Can't believe I missed all the excitement, that's
            only flippin typical of me.

CAITLIN   It felt very much as if – she wanted to get away
            from us.

MAY   Well, whatever. You know what your Mister
            Mercury says.

CAITLIN   No, what does he say?

MAY   Dun dun dun – another one bites the dust.

CAITLIN   Ah, very good.

            …

MAY   Y'all right?

CAITLIN   I'm fine.

MAY   Okay.

            MAY *takes a couple of painkillers washed down
            with the Coke.*

            (*Re: his place.*) Any sign of himself?

CAITLIN   Not yet.

MAY   Me ovaries're killin. Killin.

CAITLIN   Means they're working.

MAY   Yes yes that much is true. It's true.

            …

            You want a Coke?

CAITLIN   I'm all right.

MAY   Okay. You just say.

CAITLIN   I'm fuckin fine will ya –

            …

MAY   That's good then.

            MAY *watching* CAITLIN *for a bit on the side-eye.*

            You sit so still. It's incredible.

CAITLIN   What?

MAY   You sit. Very still.

CAITLIN   I know.

MAY   It's impressive.

CAITLIN   I used to be fat.

MAY   WHAT?

CAITLIN   I sit still cuz I used to be fat. Okay? Yes?

              MAY, *eyes popping and mouth going but saying nothing still.*

              You want to be – you make yourself less. Like, if you move less, if you make less noise, you might magically get smaller or somethin. I dunno, never went much into the science of it, but. Just so maybe they'll not see you at all. Cept when I was dancin – forgot all about all of it when I was dancin. I dunno.

              …

MAY   (*Can't help herself.*) HA! Amazing. I can't believe after all this time I'm still finding out new things about ya.

CAITLIN   As if you'd ever asked.

MAY   You're the one always tellin me to shuddup.

CAITLIN   Yappin on about yourself and your – I said as if you'd ever ASKED.

MAY   Oh jesus god I'm sorry I never asked you before if you used to be fat I didn't KNOW that was a THING we were askin.

CAITLIN   May.

MAY   I mean, if I'd only known that was on the table as a conversation-starter, we coulda done this months back.

CAITLIN   Can you not do this. Please. Tonight. Can ya not.

MAY

> MAY *waits*.

> (*Brandishing the knitting*.) I mean. What's this all
> about though?

CAITLIN

MAY   Eh? What's this? Madness.

CAITLIN   Oh that. Christ.

MAY   What is this?

> …

CAITLIN   What the fuck IS that? Knitting bollix. KNIT-
           TING. Honest to god.

MAY   (*Chucks the knitting on the floor somewhere*.)
           'Knittin.'

CAITLIN   She's doin it. Yeah. She's clickyclacky fwoopfwoop
           and I'm sayin – What're you makin? Fwoopfwoop.
           'What, Caitlin?' What the fuck are ya making.
           'I was thinkin I could' – clickyclacky – 'make us all
           something matchin, yeah.' Oh, lovely. Now let me
           have a little fuckin think here. Okay now, can you
           do, em, a scarf, do ya think? 'I'm sure I could rustle
           up something if ya like' – And I'm goin – livid, as
           you can imagine, fuckin boilin the head off me – No
           no, changed me mind, if you're doin requests, how
           about 'Kumba-fuckin-ya'? D'ya know that one?

MAY   Ya didn't.

CAITLIN   I fuckin – You think I didn't?

MAY   THAT'S MORE LIKE IT – more LIKE it, Cait.

CAITLIN   What a prick. You know? Just. Thinking knitting
           makes her so cool. Oh, such a kook she was. Livin
           right on the fuckin edge.

> …

MAY   Why'd she do it, Cait, do ya think?

CAITLIN   The pills?

MAY   Fistful of pills and just give him up.

                Over the next, MAY *gets up and folds up*
                Gráinne's chair, packing up the things quite
                ceremonially maybe in a plastic bag.

CAITLIN   She was sayin somethin about, you know your
                pretty little one we've seen a few times now?

MAY   Now that'd be little Aideen Mary Feenan, Cait.

CAITLIN   Yeah – Aideen, that's the one. So, Gráinne was
                sayin somethin about how different he is with her,
                how tender he's being now. Like, this morning,
                did ya see? He made Aideen *breakfast*, May.

MAY   I did notice that.

CAITLIN   Now that's verging on caring, isn't it? Somethin
                like – caring for her. And us watchin, and she just
                sitting there like it's the most normal thing in the
                world. And it's not normal, breakfast.

MAY   And then after that, do you remember, she was
                leavin and still wearing his old blue hoodie, and
                he let her just walk outta there, and, and he didn't
                make her take it off, but pulled up the hood and
                tight round her face and kissed the end of her nose
                so sweet?

CAITLIN   Exactly, that kinda bollix. I think Gráinne thought
                he'd stop fuckin around now. Like, maybe he's got
                to the end of the girls. And Aideen's the last one
                for him.

MAY   Don't say that, I don't like to hear it.

                …

CAITLIN   It's awful to say but I'm feelin a – sorta incredible
                overwhelming sense of relief now Gráinne's gone,
                aren't you?

MAY   I'll not miss her. She was a weak stupid selfish –
             (*Quiet*.) fucker – (*Normal voice*.) without the
             necessary. Without the –

CAITLIN   The fight.

MAY   Without the necessary fight in her. And without
             that. Well. What are we.

CAITLIN   Silly wee girlies.

MAY   Only silly wee girlies is exactly it.

             She didn't've the heart for it, Cait, did she?

CAITLIN   Sadly no.

MAY   Not like you and me.

CAITLIN   She was a weak-hearted knittin fuckin prick and
             no mistake.

MAY   Not a one.

             Settling down again.

             …

             What was the nicest thing he said to you ever?
             Can you think of it?

CAITLIN

MAY   Cuz like. I'll never forget one night and we were
             talkin and I said somethin about – 'Oh I'm probably
             being really thick, but' – and he said that I shouldn't
             talk about myself like that. He said, You're much
             smarter than you think you are, May-May.

             And he's the only one ever said anythin like that
             to me. I remember thinkin, all of a sudden thinkin,
             that what if he? That maybe he was right.

             …

CAITLIN   Good girl.

MAY   Pardon me?

CAITLIN   He said. I think he. That's the nicest thing that'd be the nicest thing he said.

MAY   Ha. Weird thing to say, no?

CAITLIN

MAY   And so what'd be the context of it, do you remember?

CAITLIN   Like –

          Shh now. Shh. There's a good girl now. Good girl. Like that it was, I think.

MAY   Weird thing to say.

CAITLIN   Oh yeah – weird one, yeah.

          …

MAY   Oh. Meant to say. Got another package. Musta come today.

CAITLIN   Yeah?

MAY   I brought it up with me.

CAITLIN   Ohrightyeahthat'sgreat.

MAY   Just left it in the hall, so.

CAITLIN   Goooood good yeah. Here they are then –

MAY   You want me to fetch it in here?

CAITLIN   NO no no. I'll get it. Don't worry yourself.

MAY   I won't then.

CAITLIN   Ah yeah, here they are.

MAY   Finally.

          …

          Sure but he's fair sprinting off there now.

CAITLIN   Got his little poop-waddle on.

MAY   He'll be wanting a shite, yeah.

CAITLIN   See – that's little Aideen back again.

MAY   Two nights running.

CAITLIN   That's somethin.

MAY   It can't really be her that's The One, can it, Cait? Not *her*.

CAITLIN   I just don't know, May. All this, it's – unprecedented.

A moment as they both consider what this might mean, waiting for her to get upstairs and into the flat.

Here she comes in now.

MAY   But she looks very nervy, doesn't she? Flittin about like that.

CAITLIN   She does look a trifle fluttery, you're right there.

What're you doin there, Aideen?

MAY   'Oh just putting the telly on, Cait. Lookin for a fillum.'

CAITLIN   Sure, Aideen, you'll need to pass your time somehow till he's finished in the jacks.

MAY   Ha – she's got the *Titanic* Special Edition out.

CAITLIN   We'll be here all night.

MAY   Was always one of me favourites, that one. (*Maybe sings a few lines of 'My Heart Will Go On'.*)

CAITLIN   God, the tragedy of it.

MAY   Uh-oh. Looks like he's still puttin his DVDs back in the wrong boxes.

CAITLIN   C'mon, you're right in me way, Aideen –

MAY   It is not *Titanic*.

CAITLIN   What is that? Porn is it now?

MAY	That's pornos, Cait. Hey, you know that even looks like –
	A moment, then CAITLIN *drops her binoculars and covers her eyes.*
CAITLIN	DEAR LORD IN HEAVEN MY EYES.
MAY	That's me is it, Cait?
CAITLIN	Oh good fuck. Good fuckin FUCK.
MAY	(*Still watching, almost hypnotised.*) Is that me?
CAITLIN	Jesus fuck –
MAY	Ah, calm down, Cait, haven't ya seen it all before.
CAITLIN	Not on that massive fuck-off telly! Have ya not seen the high-definition version of yourself?
MAY	I certainly have.
CAITLIN	Fuckin HELL.
MAY	Oh now here he comes, Cait – quick quick here he comes –
	CAITLIN *reluctantly with her binoculars again.*
	What's she searching around for there?
CAITLIN	That'll be the camera, no?
MAY	Now he's in for it!
CAITLIN	Is she – are those tears?
MAY	Boohoo for you, little Aideen.
CAITLIN	Jesus can he not turn the telly off at least?
MAY	But I look epic up there, wha.
CAITLIN	What's she sayin?
MAY	'Who's this, oh who's this beautiful, magical woman you're makin the love to here?'
CAITLIN	And she's gettin somethin out of her handbag –

MAY   Do you think she'll mace him? That'd be gas.

CAITLIN   Don't think it's – holy shit. Holy Fuckin Balls. Is
             that what I think it is?

MAY   No.

CAITLIN   (*Doing a slow clap.*) A pregnancy test. Well now.
             Aideen Mary Feenan, tou-fuckin-ché.

MAY   What're you clappin her for?

CAITLIN   It's a great move.

MAY   But she's won now!

CAITLIN   'Won'?

MAY   She's the jackpot there, no?

CAITLIN   No, May. Think about it. She already knows
             he's scum.

MAY   Oh, Cait!

CAITLIN   Exactly.

MAY   We'll keep you a spot at the window, Aideen.

CAITLIN   This is gonna fuckin destroy him.

4.

*It's kinda carnage in the flat. Chairs tipped and stuff
everywhere. The birthday banner is either gone or only held up
at one end. There's a half-hearted mixture of Hallowe'en and
Christmas decorations scattered around – someone has tried to
make an effort but the actual effect is more of a fancy-dress-
party headache than anything particularly festive. Bits of each
of the past girls are there, and now an old blue hoodie, left
behind by Aideen.*

MAY*'s holding a pair of knitting needles covered in what looks
like blood. It's up her arm as well, maybe a little on her face.
She looks proper scary.*

CAITLIN*'s got some weird enormous goggles on her head,
some industrial-looking headphones/ear-protectors round her
neck and leather gloves on her hands. She's speechless, taking
in the scene.*

CAITLIN	(*Calling.*) Aideen?
MAY	Gone, Cait. More blue flashin lights for her – hardly original was she. We're gonna get a reputation if we're not careful.
CAITLIN	AIDEEN.
	What Did You Do.
MAY	I plucked it out with my bare hands.
	And ate it.
CAITLIN	For fuck's sake, May – look at yourself – a pair of fuckin knitting needles like some – you couldn't find a coat hanger, no?
MAY	I stuck these up her and fucked em around till the little bastard dribbled out on the floor in a twisty little gobbet.
CAITLIN	Well that's disgusting.

MAY *smiles. Slowly, slowly – licks the needles, tip to base. Licks the red from her hand.*

(*As she does.*) No. (*Retches.*) JESUS.

MAY*'s giggling, she's really enjoying herself.*

You're sick. YOU'RE SICK YOU'RE SICK.

MAY   Ah, fuck up, it's fuckin ketchup. See? I didn't do anything, I never touched her.

CAITLIN   Oh no?

MAY   Smell. It's only ketchup. Your face. Only a wee jokey there.

CAITLIN   A joke, is it? Just a fuckin TRICK YOU'RE PLAYING?

MAY   Been ages since we've had a laugh, isn't it, me and you.

    …

CAITLIN   What happened to her? Truths.

MAY   Well, so – I was takin out the bins as usual (you're welcome) and one of the bags went and split itself all down the stairs, so I got some gloves and a new black bag and was pickin it all up and I seen a little paper bag all red with blood and, honestly, horrible it was. What's this? thinks I.

    And can ya think what was in that blooded paper bag, Cait?

CAITLIN   Really not in the mood, May.

MAY   Tampax, Cait. (*Gasps.*) *Secret Tampax.* Hidden away so's we wouldn't see and we'd never know.

    …

CAITLIN   Wh– Aideen's?

MAY   Not even pregnant, Cait. Not even a bit. As you know I keep a beady eye on our Tampax supply and they're all accounted for, so looks like she's been smuggling them in. Playin us for *fools*, Cait.

CAITLIN   But why would she?

MAY   Haven't we been waitin on her hand and foot, takin care of her in her sadness, offerin kinship for her broken heart? And all the while him gettin more and more desperate for her, gettin sloppy, goin through the girls faster and faster –

CAITLIN   What about the test? She had that test she showed to him, didn't she?

MAY   Well – and I'm guessin now – maybe she was lookin to trap him. Pretend she was up the pole and then – 'Oh no, tragedy it is' – lose the babby, but by then she's a ring on her finger and it's too late for him. Pretty clever when ya think about it. She'd one up on us, for sure, sittin over here flickin our beans like a pair of fuckin eejits.

    ...

CAITLIN   When did you start cursin so much and not even sayin your little 'scuse me'?

MAY   Cuz you're a fine one / to talk –

CAITLIN   Not talking about me, talking about you. You're gone different somehow.

MAY   Oh, I'm just fine, Cait.

CAITLIN   And you're not a bit concerned about her runnin on back to him.

MAY   Not with everythin I've got on her.

CAITLIN   I don't know what I'm sposed to believe any more.

MAY   Aideen was never pregnant, Cait, never was. Truths, cross me heart.

CAITLIN   I have to fuckin trust you, May

MAY   But ya still fuckin don't. Do ya.

            You don't forget me, Cait. I'm the one what's
            stayed. It's you – and me.

            A long moment.

CAITLIN   I can't stand your face. Did ya know that? You're
            so thick it makes my brain actually physically
            hum it hums with a frequency, with a pain at times
            sometimes, actually –

MAY   Don't, Cait. You don't want to.

CAITLIN   I'll admit you have your uses, I'll give you that.
            Do me shopping. Cover me breaks. And I figured
            it out early on that you'd nowhere else to go.
            Except maybe the bottom of the Liffey. Not that
            you've the heart for anything as bold as that.

MAY   I've the heart.

CAITLIN   No ya don't! Cuz you've already gave it to *him*.
            Like a little gifty with a cherry on the top there.
            Just handed it over and no questions asked – well,
            it doesn't matter what kinda man he is, does it, cuz
            you dream him desperate into something perfect
            anyway. With eyes closed tight but your legs wide
            open and smilin.

            And it makes me laugh cuz – you know what's
            funny?

MAY   What's funny.

CAITLIN   You loved him.

MAY   What did ya think I'm doin here all this time?
            Course I did. Love him now, Cait, love him still.
            Course I fuckin do. We're meant.

CAITLIN   Oh well, that's very original. Very impressive,
            what a fuckin cliché.

MAY   You don't have to be a total weirdo to be original,
            Cait.

CAITLIN   Excuse me?

MAY   You can want all the things everyone else wants
            and to be loved like everyone else is and still be
            somethin special.

CAITLIN   But you, you're nothin, May, and not even special.
            You're the kinda girl's got so little about her, so
            little soul, that when there's no one looking at ya?
            You turn to nothin.

            You let him turn you into nothin.

            See, me up here I'm stronger, I'm bigger. Bigger'n
            him. Bigger than that. You – just blinked out and
            disappeared since you've been up here.

MAY   But he still looks at me, Cait. He's kept me so he
            can look at me any time he wants, hasn't he?

CAITLIN   He taped all of them, May, not just you.

            …

MAY   All of *us*, you mean, Cait. Yeah?

CAITLIN   He didn't film me. Not me.

MAY   What? Not you?

CAITLIN   No.

MAY   Cait, Cait, Cait. Of course he filmed ya.

CAITLIN

MAY   Oh! But imagine if Aideen put you on insteada me.

            A long moment.

            I reckon he spoke about you once, to me. Spoke to
            me about some pricktease. Bout some whale.

CAITLIN   Oh, okay then. Have your fun.

MAY   No, only cuz I spose I didn't put it all together at
            first, bein I'm so thick and all. Me bobble-heading
            and mind-numbing. Takes a while sometimes. And

I'm thinkin he'd even described you to me, bit by wobbly bit, but I reckon you'd slimmed down some by the time I first met ya. Am I right?

CAITLIN   Enough. May.

MAY   Said there's this chubby aul one hunted him down on the street just outside his building there one rainy day, and he'd felt sorry she was such a – well, a chub, he'd say – and so he'd taken her out. Taken her dancin, for that's where she'd wanted to go. And apparently she was an awful dancer, like, truly a terrible dancer but she obviously had some head on her she'd a talent for it. And who'd not feel bad for someone like that? I would, I know I would.

CAITLIN

MAY   And so he'd taken her back to his, up the stairs and home – well, she'd not say the number of her own flat, and was he meant to just leave her out in the hallways? She was pretty out of it, by all accounts, ugly drunk and half a bra hangin out and half a hair coming down. He was gonna put her to bed to sleep it off but she'd grabbed him, felt him, laid her hands all over and all over him.

CAITLIN

MAY   And – in the words of your Mizz Wynette – after all, he's just a man. And what's a man to do?

CAITLIN   I said no.

MAY   What? Can't hear.

CAITLIN   I told him no.

MAY   Well – but did ya. You know? He said, she said. Who's to know, who's to say? It's very difficult, I'm sayin.

        Who's to care?

CAITLIN   Nobody. Nobody cares but me. Nobody got hurt, but me.

MAY*'s unsure for a while what to do with her
sudden and complete advantage.*

A long moment.

MAY   I didn't know it, Cait.

CAITLIN   How could you've?

MAY   I meant to bait you, I did, but only about bein fat
             and, crap at dancin – I'd never – you know I'd
             never –

CAITLIN   I know.

MAY   You never told?

CAITLIN   What's the point in tellin, do ya know?

MAY   I coulda helped ya. If you'd asked. If only you'd
             ever said. Someone could have – done something.

CAITLIN   But they never do.

             …

MAY   I mean, I knew we were lyin to each other about
             watchin over the girls but I always thought it was
             the same thing we were after, still. Always thought
             it was him we both wanted.

CAITLIN   I did want to protect you.

MAY   Okay.

CAITLIN   Just – want to hurt him more.

             …

MAY   I think you should get yourself out there again, you
             know? Not that bad – out. Once ya get used to it.

CAITLIN   Don't know, May.

MAY   Meet some people. Get a little drink, have a little
             dance.

             That kinda shite.

CAITLIN   I wouldn't know how, I don't think, any more.

Seems like such a big thing to do.

MAY   Not scared now, are ya, Cait?

CAITLIN   Me? Pff. No.

MAY   Not so scary. To want something.

CAITLIN   Says you. Hiding away up here these months.

MAY   Well. Says me.

CAITLIN   Says you.

…

MAY   He's home then.

CAITLIN   Oh yeah?

MAY   Yeah.

They're sorta casually peering through the window but don't go for their binoculars straight away.

CAITLIN   It's early, no?

MAY   Cait.

CAITLIN   Yeah.

MAY   Look, Cait.

CAITLIN   I'm lookin.

MAY   He looks so strange tonight.

…

Is he hurt or somethin?

CAITLIN   He's not hurt.

MAY   Smaller, he looks.

CAITLIN   He looks fuckin terrible, doesn't he?

MAY   He does.

CAITLIN   He looks almost like a broken man.

            …

MAY   So. He's on his own.

CAITLIN   He is.

MAY   On his own finally?

CAITLIN   Finally.

MAY   Poor boy.

CAITLIN   Poor nothin.

            So. That's the last girl gone.

MAY   We did it, Cait.

            …

CAITLIN   Hey – would you want that surprise now?

MAY   Would I ever.

CAITLIN   Wait one here.

            CAITLIN *goes out and* MAY's *left there. She's
            almost still, breathing steadily, trying to be
            cheerful and in the room for her surprise but
            unable to stop herself looking to him, thinking
            about him.*

            And CAITLIN's *coming in from the bedroom.
            She's pseudo-expertly holding some kind of crazy
            but seriously impressive-looking sniper-rifle kinda
            thing, moving military-sideways, silent. It's
            ridiculous and strangely terrifying at the same time.*

MAY   Frig me. This is what you been putting together all
            this time?

CAITLIN   Shockingly easy to put together one of these from
            parts ordered from across the darker bits of the
            internet. If you've money. If you're patient.

MAY   That's terrifyin, Cait.

CAITLIN   It's fuckin criminal, May. But, here we are. Look at her.

MAY   She's a beaut.

CAITLIN   She is.

MAY   Ya look cool with it.

CAITLIN   Yeah?

MAY   Ya look the business, like. 'I need your clothes, your boots and your motorcycle.' You know that one?

CAITLIN   Like Arnie?

MAY   Like The fuckin Terminator, Cait.

CAITLIN   Watch your language.

MAY   Scuse me.

...

You know how to use her, do ya, or am I in trouble?

CAITLIN *raises the rifle, aiming straight at* MAY.

Okay.

CAITLIN   Why would you be in trouble?

MAY   I dunno. You'd be the one with the gun.

CAITLIN   Yep.

MAY   It's a hell of a surprise.

CAITLIN   Good.

MAY   What's she for then, Cait?

CAITLIN *swings round, so the gun is pointing out the window – at us.*

Don't!

CAITLIN   Don't what?

MAY   We're safe, Cait – look! Isn't it over? You'd kill him?

CAITLIN   I always said so.

MAY   I thought we were just talking.

CAITLIN   You said you'd kill me, didn't you.

MAY   Of course I did. That's our game, isn't it, I'll kill you, you'll kill me, we all have a good old laugh.

CAITLIN

...

A phone starts to ring. They both tense up immediately. MAY *looking to* CAITLIN.

It rings and rings.

It stops.

A breathless moment. MAY *fumbles her phone out of her bag. Stares at it.*

Who was that, May?

MAY

CAITLIN   Who was it.

MAY   You'll never guess.

CAITLIN   Has he left ya a message? May? Can I see?

MAY   Do you know what this means?

CAITLIN   It means he's lonely. Means he's desperate –

MAY   He went through all them girlies and he comes back to me.

CAITLIN   Listen to yourself –

MAY   (*As the phone rings again in her hand.*) Oh jesus god –

CAITLIN   Don't. May.

MAY

CAITLIN   Don't you answer that.

They have a small, pathetic tussle where
CAITLIN *tries to take the phone and* MAY, *in*
some weird superhuman way, throws her off and
answers the phone.

MAY   Hello? (*To* CAITLIN.) It's me answerphone.

           CAITLIN *just watching as* MAY *listens, her face*
           scarily unreadable.

           MAY *hangs up.*

           They're looking straight at each other.

           CAITLIN *lifts the rifle, points it at* MAY.

           MAY *goes to her bag. Over the next she roots*
           around. Pulls out an incredible glittery scrap of
           a dress. Takes off her other clothes and puts the
           dress on. Strappy heels go on. She gets out
           a make-up bag and mirror and puts make-up on.
           All this takes as long as it takes.

CAITLIN   What the fuck are you doing, May?

MAY   What's it look like I'm doing?

CAITLIN   (*Gestures with the gun, a warning.*) MAY.

MAY   What?

           CAITLIN's *aim wavers.*

CAITLIN   You'd go back there, after all?

MAY   But haven't we seen him grow and change? Like,
           I'd say we'd taught him how to be better, hadn't
           we, maybe even a better man. The foreplay, yeah?
           – the breakfast, the tender care he's learned.

CAITLIN   No.

MAY   I reckon he's ready now for love. For me.

CAITLIN   You could have anyone, May.

MAY   Oh yeah sure.

CAITLIN   You could, you can. Any other man.

MAY   I don't want any other man. I love him, don't I.

CAITLIN   Why?

MAY   All those other boys, all those other nights, and. He's the only one really saw me. And you're right, you know, I do need to be seen. Need to be seen by him.

CAITLIN   I don't think you realise just how fuckin sad that is.

...

MAY   I like to think. If circumstances were not what they are, maybe. We coulda been mates.

CAITLIN   I don't like you, May. I'd only ever not like you.

MAY   But, like, just look at us! We could have taken over the world, you know, me and you. If we wanted. Isn't that funny?

CAITLIN   We're never ever friends.

MAY   I think that's really funny.

A strange moment between them.

You wouldn't hurt me, Cait, if I go round there? You'll give me my chance for somethin, won't you? You'll let us try for happy?

CAITLIN *hesitates and lowers the gun.*

CAITLIN   I won't shoot ya, May.

MAY*, ready now, folds up her chair maybe and picks up her stuff. She looks incredible – like a glamourpuss.*

MAY   How do I look?

She makes sure CAITLIN *gets a good look at her, then puts on her coat.*

And she's gone.

CAITLIN's very still for a while.

Then she places the rifle carefully against her chair, and runs off. Comes back on dragging a huge, black rucksack, fully half her size at least.

She hoists on the rucksack and, with difficulty now under the weight of it, picks up the rifle. She takes a silencer out of her jacket pocket, kisses it, twists it onto the end of the rifle. Turns and faces out of the window. Raises and aims.

Blackout.

And in the blackout, a weird-coloured flash and an incredibly loud gunshot.

5.

The flat itself is as we left it, but CAITLIN *is now on the floor, 'wearing' but actually laying on top of the massive rucksack like a beetle on its back, bruised face and with blood on her right cheek.* MAY *is standing over* CAITLIN, *there's blood all over her glittering dress and arms, mascara down her face.*

MAY   You didn't factor in the kickback.

CAITLIN   No, I didn't factor in the fuckin kickback.

MAY   Me ears are still ringin.

CAITLIN   Fuckin silencer flew right off like a rocket.

MAY   You're a danger to yourself, Cait.

             CAITLIN *is struggling to get up.*

             …

             You want some help there?

CAITLIN   I'm fine.

Over the next, CAITLIN *allows* MAY *to help get her arms out of the straps, maybe pulls her up.*

(*Re: blood on* MAY.) Are you okay?

MAY   It's not mine, is it.

CAITLIN   That's good.

MAY   So much of it. You see that on the films, like, but I always thought they were makin it up.

CAITLIN   Yeah?

MAY   Was like being in a film, actually. So weird, it was.

CAITLIN   Oh yeah.

MAY   Didn't even kiss him, Cait. Didn't get to touch him at all.

CAITLIN

MAY   So, there's me, I'm straight through the door and seems he does have a blind, like, if ya can believe it, so for obvious reasons I'm gone straight over to pull it down and but there *you* are – and then the world explodes.

CAITLIN   May.

MAY   (*Rummaging in her bag.*) Did get a little memento, though. (*Pulls out the* Titanic *DVD.*) But – oh no! I didn't think to look for you. (*Smacks herself on the forehead.*) Oops.

              So, yeah, so – thing is, Cait, I don't really know what to do now. Without him.

CAITLIN   You shouldn't let yourself be defined by a man like that.

MAY   Well now, I always lacked definition in the past, so I guess I just don't see it as such a bad thing. And anyway you're one to talk, if you'd look at yourself.

CAITLIN   Fair point.

              ...

MAY   You were gonna leg it on me.

CAITLIN   No.

MAY   Can't stay here, can ya? Hole in window and hole
             in him.

CAITLIN   Come on, May. *Now* it's over.

MAY   If you'd not fallen on your arse in all the
             commotion, stuck there beetling on your back,
             you'd already be gone.

             …

CAITLIN   What do you want me to say?

MAY   You can't even pretend you woulda waited for me?

CAITLIN   I've a feelin it might be too late for that.

MAY   You'll never guess but he was playing Fleetwood
             Mac when I turned up.

CAITLIN   He was?

MAY   Swear. You know the spooky one –

             *She hums or sings a bit of the verse of
             'Everywhere'.*

             Those twinklies at the start of it like somethin
             bad's gonna happen.

             …

CAITLIN   It's my name on the lease, there'll be no one
             lookin for you.

MAY   That's now that is true.

CAITLIN   Please. You can go.

MAY   Well but we'll have a goodbye hug first, won't we.

             MAY *slams into* CAITLIN *with a hug.* CAITLIN
             jerks a little. MAY *clings on to her as she speaks.*

I'm sorry, Cait. To think I almost believed you, wanted to, really did. But all this, what you just pulled? That wasn't saving anyone. Not taking back the looking, not none of that you spouted, so like a hero. But all it was the whole time: you couldn't have him, so couldn't no one else have him either. Specially not me.

MAY *releases* CAITLIN *and* CAITLIN *drops to the floor, knitting needles sticking out of her and blood pouring out.*

So see you're a horrible cliché, too.

CAITLIN *looks down at herself. Thinking about or maybe trying to think about pulling out the needles, she can't focus and her hands don't work.*

MAY *puts on her coat, covering the bloodstains on herself, checks her phone.*

Right, well, that's me, so.

Grabs hold of CAITLIN*'s rucksack and starts to drag it out after her.* CAITLIN *looks up at her, trying to work out what's happening. She's shaking, little convulsions that seem to surprise her.*

CAITLIN   Someone saw. Someone's coming.

            …

MAY   But they never ever do. You know that.

            And MAY*'s gone.*

CAITLIN   Shh. Shh. Someone. Saw.

            CAITLIN *is trying to push herself up, trying to call out, but she's too hurt, her voice is nothing.*

            The lights very gradually start to go down, maybe 'Everywhere' by Fleetwood Mac starts to play.

            Blackout.

            The End.

A Nick Hern Book

Peep first published in Great Britain in 2018 as a paperback original by Nick Hern Books Limited, The Glasshouse, 49a Goldhawk Road, London W12 8QP

Peep copyright © 2018 Jodi Gray

Jodi Gray has asserted her moral right to be identified as the author of this work

Cover image: © iStock.com/Devrimb

Designed and typeset by Nick Hern Books, London
Printed in Great Britain by Mimeo Ltd, Huntingdon, Cambridgeshire PE29 6XX

A CIP catalogue record for this book is available from the British Library

ISBN   978 1 84842 741 9

www.nickhernbooks.co.uk

facebook.com/nickhernbooks

twitter.com/nickhernbooks